BLACK EXCELLENCE

A CELEBRATION OF GREATNESS

Written By

Jelani Hashim Bracey

Illustrated By Jasmine T. Mills

To every Black child EVERYWHERE.......
Love yourself.
Love your people.
Love your culture.

Here is a powerful message to all my young Black Kings and Queens.

ALWAYS be proud of being Black, because it means EVERYTHING!

You come from a culture with a great and rich history that starts at the beginning of time.

You come from the first people to ever walk the face of the earth. The very first of humankind.

You come from the people that built The Great Pyramids; and some of the most magnificent wonders the world has ever known.

You come from great generations of powerful nations; but the worst of your past is always shown.

You come from those that first explored the skies

and mapped the stars and planets above.

So, say it loud, "I'M BLACK AND I'M PROUD!"

BLACK
IS
BEAUTIFUL

And show
yourself
much love!

You come from an AMAZING culture
full of beauty, style and grace.

A culture that has stood the test of time, with a strength and pride that cannot be erased.

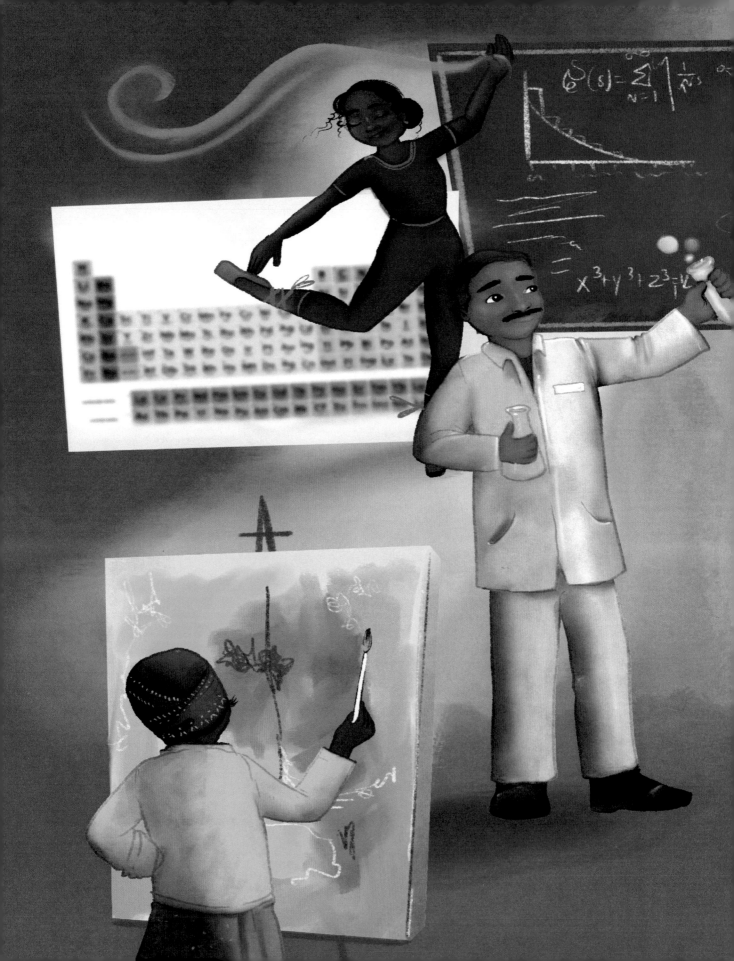

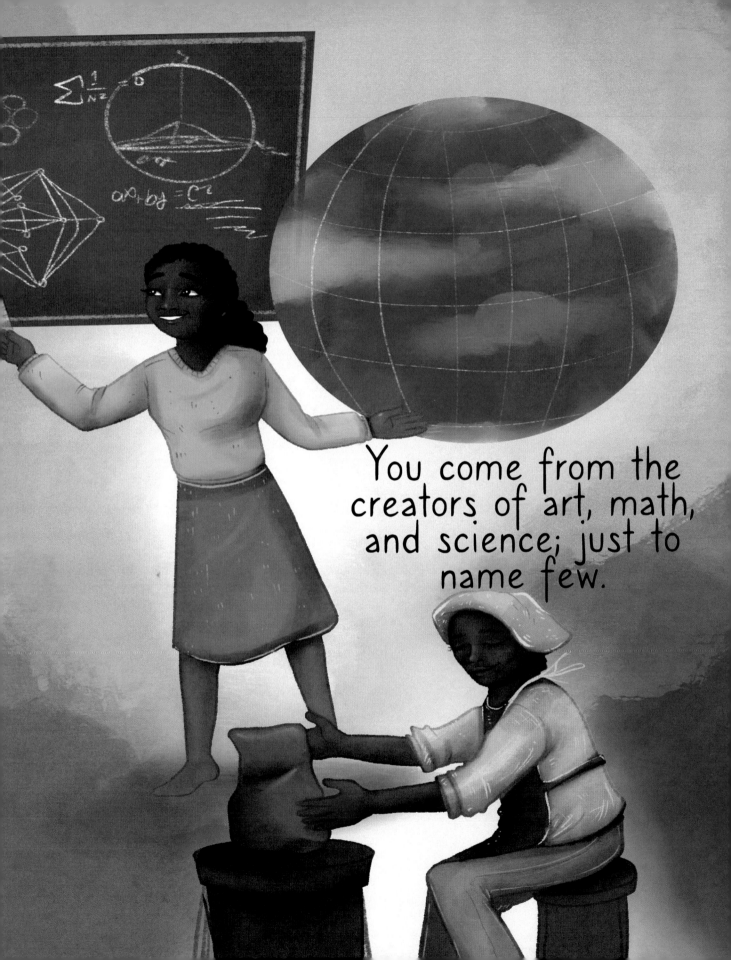

You come from the creators of art, math, and science; just to name few.

THE WORLD

So, never doubt yourself or how great you are.

IS YOURS.

There's nothing that you can't do.

You come from a people of
great wisdom and knowledge.

You are a reflection of your ancestors, so always pay homage.

You come from the very first great kings and queens of the Earth.

And from mighty and powerful warriors, so never forget your worth!

There are so many stories about Black Excellence that are ready for you to explore.

And what you find will open your mind, and you'll be ready to search for much more!

So, love yourself and
believe in who you are.

And never fold,
break or bend.

And ALWAYS be proud of being Black!

Because Black

is BEAUTIFUL!

Black is AMAZING!

The End!

10 Gifts From Black Culture to the World

1. **Math** – Africans created the earliest number system on record and were the first people to create and solve arithmetic equations. The Lebombo bone is the oldest math instrument ever found; and it dates back to 35,000 B.C. It was used for measuring and was found in the Lebombo caves of Swaziland in Southern Africa.

2. **Art** - The Blombos Cave in South Africa is home to some of the oldest prehistoric art in all of Africa. The crosshatch patterns on the walls of the cave date back to 70,000 B.C.

3. **Writing** -   The oldest form of writing is believed to be cuneiform, and it comes from the Black Sumerians of Mesopotamia (modern day Iraq). This writing system was invented about 3500 B.C. Also, Africa has the world's oldest and largest collection of written languages.

4. **Astronomy** – Many Ancient African societies had advanced knowledge of the universe and correctly plotted the stars and constellations; and tracked the orbits of the Earth, moon, and Sun throughout space. The Dogon people of Mali discovered Saturn's rings, Jupiter's moons, and the spiral structure of the Milky Way galaxy.

5. **Metallurgy** (metal making) – The earliest evidence of metal making was discovered in Sub Saharan Africa. The objects found dated back between 3000 and 2500 B.C. Ancient African advancements in metal making include steam engines, metal chisels and saws, copper and iron tools and weapons, nails, glue, carbon steel and bronze.

6. **Medicine** – medical procedures such as brain surgery, autopsy, skin grafting, caesarian births and vaccinations were all African inventions.

7. **Architecture and engineering** – massive stone complexes and castle sized buildings were created in Zimbabwe and Mozambique. The Ancient Egyptians built huge obelisks and The Great Pyramids; with the largest pyramid made of 2.25 million blocks of stone and covering 13 acres. The Empire of Mali constructed impressive cities, like Timbuktu, with grand palaces, mosques and universities.

8. **Navigation** – Ancient Africans were the first to sail to South America and Asia hundreds of years before anyone else. Many ancient societies in Africa built different types of boats from small vessels to very large ships. The Mali and Songhai Empires both built boats 100 feet long and 13 feet wide that could carry up to 80 tons

9. **Religion** – The Black Sumerians had their own Gods and Goddesses called the Annunaki. Many ancient African spiritual practices and customs have been copied by many cultures for centuries.

10. **Law** – Ancient Egyptians had laws that were based on Ma'at, which is an Ancient Egyptian concept of truth, balance, order, harmony, law, morality, and justice.

Made in the USA
Middletown, DE
07 January 2022